Teach Me...™ Everyday GERMAN

Volume 1

Written by Judy Mahoney
Illustrated by Patrick Girouard

Technology is changing our world. Far away exotic places have literally become neighbors. We belong to a global community and our children are becoming "global kids." Comparing and understanding different languages and cultures is more vital than ever! Additionally, learning a foreign language reinforces a child's overall education. Early childhood is the optimal time for children to learn a second language, and the Teach Me Everyday Language Series is a practical and inspiring way to teach them. Through story and song, each book and audio encourages them to listen, speak, read and write in a foreign language.

Today's "global kids" hold tomorrow's world in their hands. So when it comes to learning a new language, don't be surprised when they say, "teach me!"

The German taught in school is called "Hochdeutsch" or High German. At home, however, Germans may speak one of dozens of dialects from the various regions of Germany and Austria. Each dialect can sound like a completely different language; each with its own regional idiosyncrasies. Not only are vowels and consonants pronounced differently, but even entire words are enunciated differently. Fortunately, the majority of Germans are able to speak and understand Hochdeutsch.

Teach Me Everyday German
Volume One
ISBN 13: 978-1-59972-103-3
Library of Congress PCN: 2008902657

Copyright © 2008 by Teach Me Tapes, Inc.
6016 Blue Circle Drive, Minnetonka, MN 55343
www.teachmetapes.com

Book Design by Design Lab, Northfield, MN

10 9 8 7 6 5 4 3 2

INDEX & SONG LIST

Je öfter wir uns treffen 🎵🎵
Je öfter wir uns treffen, uns treffen, uns treffen,
Je öfter wir uns treffen, um so fröhlicher sind wir.
Deine Freunde sind meine Freunde
Und meine Freunde sind deine Freunde.
Je öfter wir uns treffen, um so fröhlicher sind wir.

The More We Get Together
The more we get together, together, together
The more we get together the happier we'll be
For your friends are my friends
And my friends are your friends
The more we get together the happier we'll be.

Guten Tag.
Ich heiße Maria.
Wie heißt du?

Das ist meine Familie.

Hello.
My name is Maria.
What is your name?

Here is my family.

mein Bruder

mein Vater

meine Mutter

ich

My father
My mother
My brother
I

Meine Katze.
Sie heißt Muschi.
Sie ist grau.

My cat.
Her name is Muschi.
She is gray.

meine Katze

Mein Hund.
Er heißt Spitz.
Er ist schwarz und weiß.

mein Hund

My dog.
His name is Spitz.
He is black and white.

Und das ist mein Haus. Es hat ein rotes Dach und einen Garten mit gelben Blumen.

Here is my house. It has a red roof and a garden with yellow flowers.

Mein Zimmer ist blau.
Es ist sieben Uhr.
Wach-auf! Wach-auf!

My room is blue.
It is seven o'clock.
Wake up! Wake up!

Bruder Jakob
Bruder Jakob, Bruder Jakob!
Schläfst du noch, Schläfst du noch?
Hörst du nicht die Glocken?
Hörst du nicht die Glocken?
Bim bem bam! Bim bem bam!

Are You Sleeping
Are you sleeping, are you sleeping
Brother John, Brother John
Morning bells are ringing
Morning bells are ringing
Ding dang dong! Ding dang dong!

Heute ist Montag.
Kennst du die Wochentage?
Montag, Dienstag, Mittwoch,
Donnerstag, Freitag, Samstag, Sonntag.

Today is Monday.
Do you know the days of the week?
Monday, Tuesday, Wednesday,
Thursday, Friday, Saturday, Sunday.

MONTAG
Monday

DIENSTAG
Tuesday

MITTWOCH
Wednesday

DONNERSTAG
Thursday

FREITAG
Friday

SAMSTAG
Saturday

SONNTAG
Sunday

elf

Ich ziehe mich an. Ich ziehe meine Bluse, meine Hose und meine Schuhe an. Dann setze ich meinen Hut auf.

I get dressed.
I put on my shirt,
my pants and my shoes.
Then I put on my hat.

Kopf, Schultern, Knie und Fuß
Kopf und Schultern, Knie und Fuß, Knie und Fuß.
Kopf und Schultern, Knie und Fuß, Knie und Fuß.
Augen, Nase, Ohren und Mund,
Kopf und Schultern, Knie und Fuß, Knie und Fuß. ♪

Head, Shoulders, Knees and Toes
Head and shoulders, knees and toes, knees and toes
Head and shoulders, knees and toes, knees and toes
Eyes and ears and mouth and nose
Head and shoulders, knees and toes, knees and toes.

Ich frühstücke. Ich esse gerne Brot und trinke heiße Schokolade dazu.

I eat breakfast.
I like to eat bread and
drink hot chocolate with it.

Es ist schlechtes Wetter. Es regnet. Heute kann ich nicht hinaus.

The weather is bad. It is raining.
I cannot go outside today.

Rain Medley

Rain, rain, go away
Come again another day
Rain, rain, go away
Little Johnny wants to play.

It's raining, it's pouring
The old man is snoring
He bumped his head and went to bed
And couldn't get up in the morning.

Regen, Regen

Regen, Regen, hör doch auf!
Regne auf ein anderes Haus!
Regen, Regen, hör doch auf!
Hänschen möchte spielen.

Regenbogen

Ein lichtes Blau, ein lichtes Grün
Farben hell am Himmel glüh'n
Rot und gelb, oh wie schön,
Bunter Regenbogen.

Rainbows

Sometimes blue and sometimes green
Prettiest colors, I've ever seen
Pink and purple, yellow - whee!
I love to ride those rainbows.

Das ist meine Schule.
Ich sage: "Guten Morgen,
Frau Schmoll."
Ich lerne die Zahlen
und das Alphabet.

meine Schule

Here is my school.
I say, "Good morning, Ms. Schmoll."
I learn my numbers
and my alphabet.

die Zahlen

1 **eins** (eyns)
2 **zwei** (tsvigh)
3 **drei** (dry)
4 **vier** (feer)
5 **fünf** (fuenf)
6 **sechs** (zeks)
7 **sieben** (ZEE-bin)
8 **acht** (akht)
9 **neun** (noin)
10 **zehn** (tsane)

Numbers
one two three four five six seven eight nine ten

das Alphabet

A a (ah) B b (beh) C c (ceh) D d (deh) E e (eh)

F f (eff) G g (geh) H h (haa) I i (eeh) J j (yot) K k (kaa)

L l (ell) M m (emm) N n (enn) O o (oh) P p (peh)

Q q (koo) R r (err) S s (ess) ß (ess-tsett) T t (teh) U u (ooh)

V v (fow) W w (vay) X x (ixx) Y y (ip se lon) Z z (tsett)

Nun kann ich sagen um die Wett' die Buchstaben von A bis Zet.

Alphabet

Aa Bb Cc Dd Ee Ff Gg Hh Ii
Jj Kk Ll Mm Nn Oo Pp Qq Rr
Ss ß * Tt Uu Vv Ww Xx Yy Zz
Now I know my ABC's, next time won't you sing with me.

* ß = ss

siebzehn

Marias süßes kleines Lamm

Marias süßes kleines Lamm, kleines Lamm, kleines Lamm,
Marias süßes kleines Lamm, das hatte schneeweißes Fell.
Es lief ihr immer hinterdrein, hinterdrein, hinterdrein.
Es lief ihr immer hinterdrein, lief mit auf Schritt und Tritt.

Mary Had a Little Lamb
Mary had a little lamb, little lamb, little lamb
Mary had a little lamb, its fleece was white as snow.
Everywhere that Mary went, Mary went, Mary went
Everywhere that Mary went, the lamb was sure to go.

Ein Elefant
Ein Elefant wollt' bummeln gehn,
Sich die weite Welt beseh'n.
Langsam setzt er Fuß vor Fuß,
Denn er ist kein Omnibus.

Bald ist er nicht mehr allein,
Alles trampelt hinterdrein.
Und schon singt das ganze Land.
Dieses Lied vom Elefant.

One Elephant
One elephant went out to play
Upon a spider's web one day
He had such enormous fun
That he called for another elephant to come.

Brüderchen, komm tanz mit mir

Brüderchen, komm tanz mit mir!
Beide Händchen reich' ich dir
Einmal hin, einmal her,
Rundherum das ist nicht schwer.

Mit den Füßchen trapp, trapp, trapp,
Mit den Händchen klapp, klapp, klapp,
Einmal hin, einmal her,
Rundherum das ist nicht schwer.

Brother Come Dance with Me

Brother come dance with me
Take our hands and one, two, three
Right foot first, and left foot then
Round about and back again.

With your feet, tap, tap, tap
With your hands, clap, clap, clap
Right foot first, left foot then
Round about and back again.

Nach der Schule fahren wir mit dem Auto nach Hause.

After school, we drive in our car to our house.

Die Autoräder

Die Autoräder drehen sich,
Drehen sich, drehen sich,
Die Autoräder drehen sich
Durch die ganze Stadt.

Die Autohupe macht tütüt,
Macht tütüt, macht tütüt,
Die Autohupe macht tütüt
Durch die ganze Stadt.

Die Kinder im Auto gehen nach Haus',
Gehen nach Haus', gehen nach Haus',
Die Kinder im Auto gehen nach Haus'
Durch die ganze Stadt.

The Wheels on the Car
The wheels on the car go round and round
Round and round, round and round
The wheels on the car go round and round
All around the town.

The horn on the car goes beep beep beep
Beep beep beep, beep beep beep
The horn on the car goes beep beep beep
All around the town.

The children in the car go, "Let's have lunch,
Let's have lunch, let's have lunch"
The children in the car go, "Let's have lunch"
All around the town.

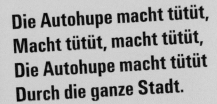

Jetzt gibt es Mittagessen.
Nach dem Essen halte ich
meinen Mittagsschlaf.

It is lunch time.
After lunch it is nap time.

Mein liebes Kindchen ♪

Mein liebes Kindchen, schlafe ein!
Papa kauft dir ein Vögelein.
Und wenn dein Vögelein nicht singt,
Kauft Papa einen Diamantenring.
Und wenn der Ring nicht glänzen will,
Kauft Papa dir einen Spiegel schnell.
Und wenn der Spiegel bricht entzwei,
Bleibst du unser liebes Kindelein.

Hush Little Baby

Hush little baby don't say a word
Papa's going to buy you a mockingbird
If that mockingbird won't sing
Papa's going to buy you a diamond ring
If that diamond ring turns brass
Papa's going to buy you a looking glass
If that looking glass falls down
You'll still be the sweetest little baby in town.

Nach dem Mittagsschlaf gehen wir in den Park. Dort sehe ich viele Enten. Ich singe und tanze mit meinen Freunden auf der Brücke.

After our naps, we go to the park. I see the ducks. I sing and dance with my friends on the bridge.

Auf der Brücke von Avignon

Auf der Brücke von Avignon
Tanzen alle, tanzen alle.
Auf der Brücke von Avignon
Tanzen alle im Kreis herum.

On the Bridge of Avignon
On the Bridge of Avignon
They're all dancing, they're all dancing
On the bridge of Avignon
They're all dancing round and round.

Sechs kleine Enten

Sechs kleine Enten, die ich einmal sah,
Dicke, dünne und auch hübsche waren da,
Doch die eine Ente mit 'ner
Feder auf dem Rücken
Führte alle an mit ihrem quak quak quak,
Quak quak quak, quak quak quak,
Führte alle an mit ihrem quak quak quak.

Six Little Ducks

Six little ducks that I once knew
Fat ones, skinny ones, fair ones, too
But the one little duck
With the feather on his back
He led the others with his quack quack quack
Quack quack quack, quack quack quack
He led the others with his quack quack quack.

Hänschen klein

Hänschen klein, ging allein, in die weite Welt hinein.
Stock und Hut steh'n ihm gut, ist gar wohlgemut.
Aber Mutter weinet sehr, hat ja nun kein Hänschen mehr.
Hänschen klein, ging allein, in die weite Welt hinein.

Little John

Little John, went alone out into the wide world
With his walking stick and hat, he is happy
But mother cries because she lost her little John.
Little John went alone out into the world.

Ich habe Hunger.
Es gibt Abendessen.

I am hungry.
It is dinner time.

Oh! Susanna

Ich komm' von Alabama
Mit dem Banjo auf dem Knie.
Ich geh' nach Louisiana, meinen Schatz Susann ich seh'.
Oh, Susanna, ach, weine nicht um mich!
Ich komm' von Alabama
Mit dem Banjo auf dem Knie.

Oh! Susanna
Well, I come from Alabama
With a banjo on my knee
I'm going to Louisiana, my true love for to see
Oh, Susanna, won't you cry for me
'Cause I come from Alabama
With a banjo on my knee.

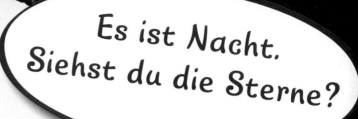

Es ist Nacht. Siehst du die Sterne?

It is night time.
Do you see the stars?

Siehst du die vielen Sterne steh'n

Siehst du die vielen Sterne steh'n?
Die hoch am Himmel sind zu seh'n?
Dunkel ist es in der Nacht,
Doch morgen kommt ein neuer Tag.
Ich freu' mich, wenn die Sonne lacht
Und ich am Morgen froh erwach'.

Twinkle, Twinkle
Twinkle, twinkle, little star
How I wonder what you are
Up above the world so high
Like a diamond in the sky
Twinkle, twinkle, little star
How I wonder what you are.

Schlaf, Kindlein
Schlaf, Kindlein, schlaf!
Der Vater hüt' die Schaf.
Die Mutter schüttelt's Bäumelein,
Da fällt herab ein Träumelein,
Schlaf, Kindlein, schlaf!

German Lullaby
Sleep, children, sleep
The father guards the sheep
The mother shakes the dreamland tree
And from it falls sweet dreams for thee
Sleep, children, sleep.

Goodnight, Mommy.
Goodnight, Daddy.
I love you very much.
Goodnight my friends,
goodnight.

Gute Nacht meine Freunde

Gute Nacht, meine Freunde, gute Nacht!
Gute Nacht, meine Freunde, gute Nacht!
Gute Nacht, meine Freunde, gute Nacht!
Gute Nacht, meine Freunde, gute Nacht!
Gute Nacht!

Goodnight My Friends

Goodnight, my friends, goodnight
Goodnight, my friends, goodnight
Goodnight, my friends
Goodnight, my friends
Goodnight, my friends, goodnight.
Goodnight!

Möchtest du mehr lernen?
(Want to learn more?)

die Lampe

das Banjo

die Couch

der Ball

der Hund

das Kissen

das Fenster

das Bett

die Puppe

der heiße Kakao

die heiße Schokolade

das Brot

die Marmelade

der Baum

die Freundin

die Brücke

der Fußball

die Farben

rot
violett
blau
grün
orange
grau
gelb
rosa
braun
weiß
schwarz